Frederick Douglass

by Lola M. Schaefer

Consulting Editor: Gail Saunders-Smith, Ph.D.

Consultant: Thomas J. Davis, Ph.D., J.D., Professor,
Department of History, College of Law,
Arizona State University

Pebble Books

an imprint of Capstone Press
Mankato, Minnesota

Pebble Books are published by Capstone Press
151 Good Counsel Drive, P.O. Box 669, Mankato, Minnesota 56002
http://www.capstone-press.com

Copyright © 2002 Capstone Press. All rights reserved.
No part of this publication may be reproduced in whole or in part, or stored in a
retrieval system, or transmitted in any form or by any means, electronic, mechanical,
photocopying, recording, or otherwise, without written permission of the publisher.
For information regarding permission, write to Capstone Press,
151 Good Counsel Drive, P.O. Box 669, Dept. R, Mankato, Minnesota 56002.
Printed in the United States of America.

2 3 4 5 6 07 06 05 04 03 02

Library of Congress Cataloging-in-Publication Data
Schaefer, Lola M., 1950–
    Frederick Douglass / by Lola M. Schaefer.
    p. cm.—(First biographies)
    Includes bibliographic references and index.
    Summary: A simple biography of the man who, after escaping slavery, became
an orator, writer, and leader in the anti-slavery movement in the nineteenth century.
    ISBN 0-7368-1174-5 (hardcover)
    ISBN 0-7368-9370-9 (paperback)
    1. Douglass, Frederick, 1817?–1895—Juvenile literature. 2. African American
abolitionists—Biography—Juvenile literature. 3. Abolitionists—United States—
Biography—Juvenile literature. 4. Antislavery movements—United States—
History—19th century—Juvenile literature. [1. Douglass, Frederick, 1817?–1895.
2. Abolitionists. 3. African Americans—Biography.] I. Title. II. Series.
E449.D75 S33 2002
973.8′092—dc21   2001004833

Note to Parents and Teachers

The First Biographies series supports national history standards
for units on people and culture. This book describes and illustrates
the life of Frederick Douglass. The photographs support early
readers in understanding the text. This book also introduces early
readers to subject-specific vocabulary words, which are defined in
the Words to Know section. Early readers may need assistance to
read some words and to use the Table of Contents, Words to
Know, Read More, Internet Sites, and Index/Word List sections
of the book.

Table of Contents

Early Life 5

Fighting for Freedom 15

Ending Slavery 19

Words to Know 22

Read More 23

Internet Sites 23

Index/Word List 24

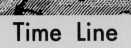

Time Line

around 1818
born

Frederick Bailey was born around 1818. He was a slave in the Southern state of Maryland. Frederick began to work at about age 8.

 a slave cabin

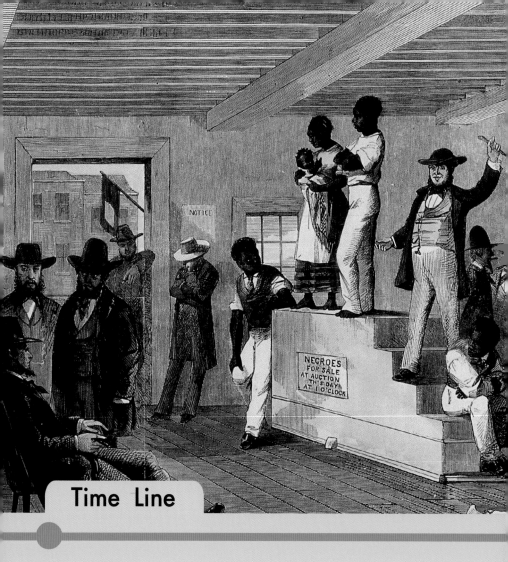

Time Line

around 1818
born

A slave's life was hard. Frederick's masters beat him and the other slaves. Masters took children from mothers and sold them. Frederick thought slavery was wrong.

a slave sale in Virginia

Time Line

around 1818
born

late 1820s
learns to
read

Frederick learned to read.

He read that some slaves bought their freedom.

He read that other slaves escaped to freedom.

Frederick wanted to be free.

Sophia Auld, a slave owner, teaching Frederick to read

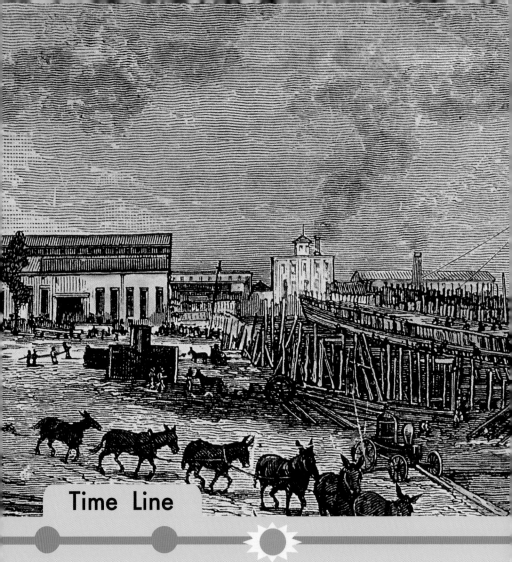

Time Line

around 1818
born

late 1820s
learns to
read

1835
plans escape

In 1835, Frederick planned to escape. But his master discovered the plan. His master made him work in a shipyard in Baltimore. Frederick met Anna Murray. She was a free black woman.

a New England shipyard

Time Line

around 1818
born

late 1820s
learns to
read

1835
plans escape

1838
escapes

Anna helped Frederick escape to New York in 1838.
New York and other Northern states had laws against keeping slaves. He changed his last name to Douglass so his master could not find him.

Anna Murray Douglass

Time Line

around 1818
born

late 1820s
learns to
read

1835
plans escape

1838
escapes;
marries
Anna Murray

Frederick and Anna got married in 1838. In 1841, Frederick began to work for the American Anti-Slavery Society. He gave speeches about the unfairness of slavery.

Frederick speaking at an anti-slavery meeting

1841
begins giving speeches against slavery

NARRATIVE

OF THE

LIFE

OF

FREDERICK DOUGLASS,

AN

AMERICAN SLAVE.

WRITTEN BY HIMSELF.

BOSTON:
PUBLISHED AT THE ANTI-SLAVERY OFFICE,
No. 25 CORNHILL.
1846.

Time Line

| around 1818 born | late 1820s learns to read | 1835 plans escape | 1838 escapes; marries Anna Murray |

In 1845, Frederick wrote his story of living as a slave. He went to England to tell people about slavery in the United States. Two Englishmen bought Frederick's freedom from his master in 1846.

a page from the book Frederick wrote

1841
begins giving speeches against slavery

1846
freedom is bought from master

Time Line

around 1818
born

late 1820s
learns to
read

1835
plans escape

1838
escapes;
marries
Anna Murray

In 1847, Frederick returned to the United States to fight slavery. Frederick wrote letters to President Lincoln. He asked the president to make slavery illegal in all states.

President Abraham Lincoln

1841
begins giving speeches against slavery

1846
freedom is bought from master

1847
returns to United States

Time Line

| around 1818 | late 1820s | 1835 | 1838 |
| born | learns to read | plans escape | escapes; marries Anna Murray |

In 1865, the U.S. Congress passed the 13th Amendment. This law freed all slaves. Frederick Douglass died in 1895. He worked his whole life for African American freedom.

◀ Frederick Douglass (right) with his grandson Joseph

1841	1846	1847	1895
begins giving speeches against slavery	freedom is bought from master	returns to United States	dies

Words to Know

amendment—a change to a law or document

American Anti-Slavery Society—an organized group of people that fought against slavery; the American Anti-Slavery Society hired Frederick Douglass to travel and to speak against slavery.

England—a country in Europe; England is part of the United Kingdom.

escape—to break free from someplace

freedom—the right to live the way you want

illegal—against the law

master—a person who owns slaves

President Lincoln—the 16th president of the United States; Abraham Lincoln was president from 1861 to 1865.

shipyard—a place where workers build ships

slave—a person owned by another person; slaves were not free to choose their homes or jobs.

U.S. Congress—a part of the government in the United States; Congress makes laws.

Read More

Becker, Helaine. *Frederick Douglass.* The Civil War. Woodbridge, Conn.: Blackbirch Press, 2001.

Douglass, Frederick. *Escape from Slavery: The Boyhood of Frederick Douglass in His Own Words.* Edited by Michael McCurdy. New York: Knopf, 1994.

McLoone, Margo. *Frederick Douglass: A Photo-Illustrated Biography.* Mankato, Minn.: Bridgestone Books, 1997.

Internet Sites

American Visionaries: Frederick Douglass
http://www.cr.nps.gov/museum/exhibits/douglass

Frederick Douglass
http://www.brightmoments.com/
blackhistory/nfdougla.html

Frederick Douglass: Abolitionist
http://www.galegroup.com/free_resources/bhm/bio/
douglass_f.htm

Index/Word List

Baltimore, 11
bought, 9, 17
children, 7
England, 17
escape, 9,
  11, 13
free, 9, 11
freedom, 9,
  17, 21
illegal, 19
law, 13, 21
letters, 19

Maryland, 5
master, 7, 11,
  13, 17
mothers, 7
New York, 13
read, 9
shipyard, 11
slave, 5, 7, 9,
  13, 17, 21
slavery, 7, 15,
  17, 19
speeches, 15

story, 17
unfairness, 15
United States,
  17, 19
U.S. Congress,
  21
woman, 11
work, 5, 11,
  15, 21
wrote, 17, 19

Word Count: 257
Early-Intervention Level: 24

Editorial Credits
Martha E. H. Rustad, editor; Heather Kindseth, cover designer and illustrator; Linda Clavel, illustrator; Kimberly Danger, Mary Englar, and Jo Miller, photo researchers

Photo Credits
CORBIS, cover, 18, 20
Howard University Archives/Moorland Spingarn Research Center, 12
National Portrait Gallery, Smithsonian Institution/Art Resource, NY, 16
The Granger Collection, New York, 14
North Wind Picture Archives, 1, 4, 6, 10
Stock Montage, 8, 16 (inset)